LAWRENCE FERLINGHETTI

POETRY AS INSURGENT ART

A NEW DIRECTIONS BOOK

Manufactured in the United Sates of America
New Directions Books are printed on acid-free paper.
First published clothbound by New Directions in 2007
Book design by Sylvia Frezzolini Severance &
Lawrence Ferlinghetti

Library of Congress Cataloging-in-Publication Data
Ferlinghetti, Lawrence.
Poetry as insurgent art / by Lawrence Ferlinghetti.
p. cm.
"A New Directions Book."
Includes bibliographical references.
ISBN 978-0-8112-1719-4 (acid-free paper)
I. Title.
PS3511.E557P56 2007
811'.54—dc22
2007011396

7 9 10 8 6

New Directions Books are published for James Laughlin
by New Directions Publishing Corporation
80 Eighth Avenue, New York 10011

CONTENTS

To Nancy Joyce Peters

POETRY AS
INSURGENT ART

The woods of Arcady are dead,
And over is their antique joy;
Of old the world on dreaming fed;
Grey truth is now her painted toy...
                                    —William Butler Yeats

What times are these
When to write a poem about love
Is almost a crime
Because it contains
So many silences
About so many horrors....
                                    —After Bertolt Brecht

"We apologize for the inconvenience,
but this is a revolution."
                                    —Subcomandante Marcos

I am signaling you through the flames.

The North Pole is not where it used to be.

Manifest Destiny is no longer manifest.

Civilization self-destructs.

Nemesis is knocking at the door.

What are poets for, in such an age? What is the use of poetry?

The state of the world calls out for poetry to save it. (A voice in the wilderness!)

If you would be a poet, create works capable of answering the challenge of apocalyptic times, even if this means sounding apocalyptic.

You are Whitman, you are Poe, you are Mark Twain, you are Emily Dickinson and Edna St. Vincent Millay, you are Neruda and Mayakovsky and Pasolini, you are an American or a non-American, you can conquer the conquerors with words.

If you would be a poet, write living newspapers. Be a reporter from outer space, filing dispatches to some supreme managing editor who believes in full disclosure and has a low tolerance for bullshit.

If you would be a poet, experiment with all manner of poetics, erotic broken grammars, ecstatic religions, heathen outpourings speaking in tongues, bombast public speech, automatic scribblings, surrealist sens- ings, streams of consciousness, found sounds, rants and raves—to create your own limbic, your own underlying voice, your *ur* voice.

If you call yourself a poet, don't just sit there. Poetry is not a sedentary occupation, not a "take your seat" practice. Stand up and let them have it.

Have wide-angle vision, each look a world glance. Express the vast clarity of the outside world, the sun that sees us all, the moon that strews its shadows on us, quiet garden ponds, willows where the hidden thrush sings, dusk falling along the riverrun, and the great spaces that open out upon the sea . . . high tide and the heron's call. . . . And the people, the people, yes, all around the earth, speaking Babel tongues. Give voice to them all.

You must decide if bird cries are cries of ecstasy or cries of despair, by which you will know if you are a tragic or a lyric poet.

If you would be a poet, discover a new way for mortals to inhabit the earth.

If you would be a poet, invent a new language anyone can understand.

If you would be a poet, speak new truths that the world can't deny.

If you would be a great poet, strive to transcribe the consciousness of the race.

Through art, create order out of the chaos of living.

Make it new news.

Write beyond time.

Reinvent the idea of truth.

Reinvent the idea of beauty.

In first light, wax poetic. In the night, wax tragic.

Listen to the lisp of leaves and the ripple of rain.

Put your ear to the ground and hear the turning of the earth, the surge of the sea, and the laments of dying animals.

Conceive of love beyond sex.

Question everything and everyone, including Socrates, who questioned everything.

Question "God" and his buddies on earth.

Be subversive, constantly questioning reality and the status quo.

Strive to change the world in such a way that there's no further need to be a dissident.

Hip Hop and Rap your way to liberation.

Try being a singing animal turned pimp for a pacifist king.

Read between the lives and write between the lines.

Your poems must be more than want ads for broken hearts.

A poem must sing and fly away with you or it's a dead duck with a prose soul.

A lyric poem must rise beyond sounds found in alphabet soup.

Write down the words of astronomers who have seen, with Heinrich Olber, the place where all is light.

Remember that "The night, a few stars" has more poetic force than a whole catalog of the heavens.

Your images in a poem should be *jamais vu*, not *déjà vu*.

Words can save you where guns can't.

Decide if a poem is a question or a declaration, a meditation or an out-cry.

Reinvent America and the world.

Climb the Statue of Liberty.

Mistrust metaphysics, trust in the imagination and re-fertilize it.

Instead of trying to escape reality, plunge into the flesh of the world.

If you call yourself a poet, sing it, don't state it.

Don't let it be said of you that sluggish imagination drowned out the slush of your heart.

Bring together again the telling of a tale and the living voice.

Be a teller of great tales, even the darkest.

Give a voice to the tongueless street.

Make common words uncommon.

Have a lover's quarrel with man's fate.

Kiss the mirror and write on it what you see and hear.

Poet, be God's spy, if God exists. Painter, paint his eye, if He has one.

Be a dark barker before the tents of existence.

See the rose through world-colored glasses.

Be an eye among the blind.

Dance with wolves and count the stars, including the ones whose light hasn't got here yet.

Be naive, non-cynical, as if you had just landed on earth, astonished by what you have fallen upon.

Question with a pure heart the inscrutable meaning of things and our tragicomic destiny.

Are you gifted with enchantment and girded with wonder? Do you have the mad sound? Be a Zen-fool.

The sunshine of poetry casts shadows. Paint them too.

You can never see or hear or feel too much. If you can stand it.

Strive to recover the innocence of eye you had in childhood.

Compose on the tongue, not on the page.

Like a Buddhist, listen to your own breathing.

Lower your voice and speak from your chest, not through your nose.

When performing your poetry, don't try to shatter windows in the next zip code.

In this art, you have no singing master, save your inner ear.

You are only as great as your ear. Too bad if it is tin.

As with humans, poems have fatal flaws.

Sing *Hello!*

Write an endless poem about your life on earth or elsewhere, a poetry larger than life.

One great poem should be born of the sum of all your poems, recording more than surface reality, more than "what's passing by the window."

Find the further reality, if there is one.

Your language must sing, with or without rhyme, to justify it being in the typography of poetry.

Make it more than "spoken word" poetry; make it "sung word" poetry.

Back up your voice with a musical instrument or other sound and let your poems blossom into song.

Dig folk singers who are the true singing poets of yesterday and today.

Read between the lines of human discourse.

Make your mind learn its way around the heart.

Your life is your poetry. If you have no heart, you'll write heartless poetry.

Avoid the provincial, go for the universal.

Don't hew stones. Dip into the sea for poetry, every poem a live fish.

Say the unsayable, make the invisible visible.

Think subjectively, write objectively.

Be a literalist of the imagination. The concrete is most poetic.

Think long thoughts in short sentences.

If you would be a poet, don't think quirks of thought are poetry.

Any three lines do not a haiku make. It takes an epiphany to make it pop.

After a poetry reading, never submit to a Question-and-Answer session. Poetry gets the listeners high. A Q-and-A brings it all down to prose. Do they ask a folk singer to explain his songs?

Like a field of sunflowers, a poem should not have to be explained.

If a poem has to be explicated, it's a failure in communication.

A poet should not discuss the craft of poetry or the process of creating it. It is more than a trade secret, mystifying by its mysteries.

Whatever a poet says *about* his work is an apology he shouldn't make.

Do you want to be a great writer or a great academic, a bourgeois poet or a flaming rad?

Can you imagine Shelley attending a poetry workshop?

Yet poetry workshops may create communities of poetic kinship in heartland America where many may feel lonely and lost for lack of kindred souls.

If you have to teach poetry, strike your blackboard with the chalk of light.

No ideas but in the senses. *Nihil in intellectu quod non prius in sensu.*

If you would be a great poet, associate with thinking poets. They're hard to find.

Thinking poetry need not be sans ecstasy.

Read the epic novelists, the prophetic poets, the great storytellers, the great minds.

Haunt bookstores.

What's on your mind? What do you

have in mind? Open your mouth and stop mumbling.

Don't be so open-minded that your brains fall out.

Become a new mind and make it newer.

Sweep away the cobwebs.

Cultivate dissidence and critical thinking. First thought may be worst thought.

Pursue the White Whale but don't harpoon it. Catch its song instead.

Allow yourself dazzling flight—flights of outrageous imagination.

Exceed everyone's great expectations and direst prophecies.

If you would be a great poet, be the conscience of the race.

Resist much, obey less.

Challenge capitalism masquerading as democracy.

Challenge all political creeds, including radical populism and hooligan socialism.

Consider Sufism, especially its tantric ecstasy in which poetry on the tongue leads to the heart and so to the soul.

Glory in the pessimism of the intellect and the optimism of the will.

Don't blow bubbles of despair.

Poetry is seeds and buds, not twigs.
Smoke it to get high.

Generate collective joy in the face of
collective gloom.

Secretly liberate any being you see in
a cage.

Liberate have-nots and enrage despots.

Sound a barbarous yawp over the
roofs of the world.

Caw the great Caw.

Sow your poems with the salt of the
earth.

Stand up for the stupid and crazy.

See eternity in the eyes of animals.

See eternity, not the other night, but tonight.

Express the inexpressible.

Don't be too arcane for the man in the street.

Be a songbird, not a parrot.

Be a canary in the coal mine. (A dead canary is not just an ornithological problem.)

Be also a rooster, waking up the world.

Write short poems in the voice of birds.

Birdsong is not made by machines. Give your poem wings to fly to the treetops.

Don't pander, especially not to audiences, readers, editors, or publishers.

Don't cater to the Middle Mind of America nor to consumer society. Be a poet, not a huckster.

Don't put down the scholastics who say a poem should have wholeness, harmony, radiance, truth, beauty, goodness.

Go to sea in ships, or work near water, and paddle your own boat.

Why listen to critics who have not themselves written great master-pieces?

Don't produce poetry by the Pound.

Don't write re-runs of virtual realities.

Be a wolf in the sheepfold of silence.

Don't slip on the banana peel of nihilism, even while listening to the roar of Nothingness.

Fill the dark abyss that yawns behind every face, every life, every nation.

Make a new poem out of every experience and overcome the myopia of the present moment.

Catch instants, every second a heart-
beat.

Stash your sell-phone and be here
now.

Look for the permanent in the
evanescent and fleeting.

Make permanent waves, and not just
on the heads of stylish women.

Don't fiddle with your moustache in
hopeless cellars, writing incompre-
hensible drivel.

Why live in the shadows? Get yourself a seat in the Sun Boat.

Don't let them tell you poetry is
bullshit.

Don't let them tell you poetry is for the birds.

Have a good laugh at those who tell you poets are misfits or potential terrorists and a danger to the state.

Don't let them tell you poetry is a neurosis that some people never outgrow.

Laugh at those who tell you poetry is all written by the Holy Ghost and you're just a ghost-writer.

Don't ever believe poetry is irrelevant in dark times.

Don't let them tell you poets are *parasiti*.

Laugh at those who tell you poetry is paid for by Social Insecurity.

Don't believe them when they tell you nobody buys the penny stock of poetry in the stock market of our casino culture.

Unless you have an urge to *sing,* don't open your mouth.

If you have nothing to say, don't say it.

Don't lecture like this. Don't say Don't.

Mock those who tell you you're living in a dream world. Dream your own reality. Camp out on the shores of reality.

Laugh at those who tell you "Go prose, young man, go prose."

Come out of your closet. It's dark in there.

Dare to be a *non-violent* poetic guerrilla, an anti-hero.

Temper your most intemperate voice with compassion.

Make new wine out of the grapes of wrath.

Remember that men & women are infinitely ecstatic, infinitely suffering beings.

Raise the blinds, throw open your shuttered windows, raise the roof, unscrew the locks from the doors, but don't throw away the screws.

Don't destroy the world unless you have something better to replace it.

Challenge Nemesis, the vengeful goddess, the invidious goddess.

Be committed to something outside yourself.

Be passionate about it.

If you would snatch fame from the flames, where is your burning bow, where your arrows of desire, where your wit on fire?

When the poet lets down his pants, his 'arse poetica' should be evident, giving rise to lyric erections.

The master class starts wars; the lower

classes fight them. Governments lie. The voice of the government is often not the voice of the people.

Speak up. Act out. Silence is complicity.

Be the gadfly of the state and also its firefly.

And if you have two loaves of bread, do as the Greeks did—sell one and with the coin of the realm buy sunflowers.

Wake up, the world's on fire!

Have a nice day.

* * *

Oh you gatherer
    of the fine ash of poetry
        ash of the too-white flame
            of poetry
Consider those who have burned
    before you
        in the so white fire
Crucible of Keats and Campana
    Bruno and Sappho
        Rimbaud and Poe and Corso
And Shelley burning on the beach
        at Viareggio

And now in the night
    in the general conflagration
      the white light
        still consuming us
    small clowns
      with our little tapers
        held to the flame!

* * *

WHAT IS POETRY?

Love lie with me
And I will tell.

Poetry is what we would cry out upon coming to ourselves in a dark wood in the middle of the journey of our life.

Poems are burning bows, poems are arrows of desire, poetry gives words to the heart.

Poetry is the truth that reveals all lies, the face without mascara.

What is poetry? Wind stirs the grasses, howls in the passes.

Voice lost and dreaming, door floated over the horizon.

O drunk flute O golden mouth, kiss kiss in stone boudoirs.

What is poetry? A clown laughs, a clown weeps, dropping his mask.

Poetry is the Unknown Guest in the house.

Poetry is the Great Memory, every word a live metaphor.

Poetry the eye of the heart, the heart of the mind.

Words wait to be reborn in the shadow of the lamp of poetry.

First light and a dark bird wings away—it's a poem.

The morning dove mourning night is my delight.

Poems are e-mails from the unknown beyond cyberspace.

Poetry is the ultimate inner refuge.

Poems are lumina, emitting light.

Poetry as an anchor in your life is only as good as the depths it can reach.

Poetry as a first language before writing still sings in us, a mute music, an inchoate music.

Life lived with poetry in mind is itself an art.

Poems like moths press against the window, trying to reach the flame.

Poetry the cry of the heart that awakens angels and kills devils.

Poetry is white writing on black, black writing on white.

Poems hide in night skies, in broken tenements, in autumn's wind-swept leaves, in lost and found letters, faces lost in a crowd. . . .

Poetry can be the bluegrass of literature, recalling us to down-home beginnings.

Poetry the painting of states of mind and deep profiles of faces.

Poetry a naked woman, a naked man, and the distance between them.

Poetry the supreme fiction.

Poetry is news from the growing edge on the far frontiers of consciousness.

Poetry a mute melody in the head of every dumb animal.

Poetry a descant rising out of the dumb heart of darkness.

It is private solitude made public.

It is the light at the end of the tunnel and the darkness within.

It is the morning dove mourning love, and nothing cries out like the cry of the heart.

Poetry holds death at bay.

Poetry is not all heroin horses and Rimbaud. It is also the powerless prayers of airline passengers fastening their seatbelts for the final descent.

Poems fulfill longings and put life back together again.

Poetry the shortest distance between two humans.

Every bird a word, every word a bird.

And every poem an exaggeration, understated.

Poetry a precession of waterbirds in flight mixed with motor accidents.

Poetry is boat-tailed birds singing in the setting sun on the tops of jacaranda trees in the plaza of San Miguel de Allende.

And all the birds of the universe flocking together in one huge book.

A poem is a phosphorescent instant illuminating time.

Poetry is more than painting sunlight on the side of a house.

The impossible function of poetry is to fathom man's destiny and transcend it.

Poetry is Van Gogh's ear echoing with all the blood of the world.

Poetry the primary conductor of emotion.

It is a lightning rod transmitting epiphanies.

It is not a spent light, a burned-out lamp, a *lume spento.*

It is a dragonfly catching fire.

It is a firefly of the imagination.

It is the sea-light of Greece, the diamond light of Greece.

Poetry is a bright vision made dark, a darkling vision made bright.

It is what the early spring is saying about the deaths of winter.

It is a black kid dancing around a banana tree at night in a patio on Toulouse Street.

Poetry is eternal graffiti in the heart of everyone.

It is the solace of the lonely—loneliness itself poetic.

Words on a page of poetry are a code for human emotions.

Paper may burn but words will escape.

A poem is a mirror walking down a high street full of visual delight.

Poetry is the shook foil of the imagination. It can shine out and half blind you.

It is the sun streaming down in the meshes of morning.

It is white nights and mouths of desire.

A poem is a tree with live leaves made from log piles of words.

A poem should arise to ecstasy somewhere between speech and song.

It is the still sound between the strings of an old violin played in the backyard of a tenement at nightfall.

Poetry is the essence of ideas before they are distilled into thought.

Poetry is a quiver on the skin of eternity.

It is made by dissolving halos in oceans of sound.

It is the street talk of angels and devils.

It is a sofa full of blind singers who have put aside their canes.

Poems are lifesavers when your boat capsizes.

Poetry is the anarchy of the senses making sense.

Poetry is all things born with wings that sing.

Poetry is a voice of dissent against the waste of words and the mad plethora of print.

It is what exists between the lines.

A true poem can create a divine stillness in the world.

It is made with the syllables of dreams.

It is far far cries upon a beach at nightfall.

It is a lighthouse moving its megaphone over the sea.

It is a picture of Ma in her Woolworth bra looking out a window into a secret garden.

It is an Arab carrying colored rugs and birdcages through the streets of Baghdad.

A poem can be made of common household ingredients. It fits on a single page yet it can fill a world and fits in the pocket of a heart.

The poet a street singer who rescues the alleycats of love.

The poet's voice is the other voice asleep in every human.

Poetry is pillow-thought after intercourse.

Poems are the lost pages of day & night.

It is the distillation of articulate animals calling to each other across a great gulf.

It is a pulsing fragment of the inner life, an untethered music.

It is the dialogue of naked statues to the sound of gaiety and weeping.

It is the sound of summer in the rain and of people laughing behind closed shutters down an alley at night.

It is Helen's straw hair in sunlight.

It is Ulysses' sword on fire.

It is a bare light bulb in a homeless hotel illuminating a nakedness of minds and hearts.

Poetry is worth nothing and therefore priceless.

It shimmers in the cup of morning.

Poetry is the incomparable lyric intelligence brought to bear upon fifty-seven varieties of experience.

It is the energy of the soul, if soul exists.

It is a high house echoing with all the voices that ever said anything crazy or wonderful.

It is a subversive raid upon the forgotten language of the collective unconscious.

Poetry a life-giving weapon deployed in the killing fields.

Poetry the perfume of resistance.

Poetry a perpetual revolt against silence exile and cunning.

Poetry deconstructs power. Absolute poetry deconstructs absolutely.

It is a real canary in a coal mine, and we know why the caged bird sings.

It is a rope to tie around you in a sounding sea without shores.

It is the shadow cast by our street-light imaginations.

Poetry is made of night-thought. If it can tear itself away from illusion, it will not be disowned before the dawn.

On the lips of the beloved, poetry is a divine pearl.

Poetry is made by evaporating the liquid laughter of youth.

Poetry is a book of light at night, dispersing clouds of unknowing.

It hears the whisper of elephants.

It knows how many angels & demons dance on the head of a phallus.

It is a humming a keening a laughing a sighing at dawn, a wild soft laughter.

It is the final gestalt of the imagination.

Poetry should be emotion recollected in emotion.

Poetry the underwear of the soul.

Words are living fossils. The poet pieces the wild beast together.

Prose masquerading in the typography of poetry is not poetry.

Poetry is not a "product." It is itself an elementary particle.

Poetry is a guillotine for accepted ideas, *des idées reçues.*

The poet a pickpocket of reality.

Poetry is a paper boat on the flood of spiritual desolation.

Poetry is madness and erotic bliss.

Poetry is the rediscovery of the self against the tribe.

The poet is the master ontologist, constantly questioning existence and reinventing it.

A poem is a flower of an instant in eternity.

The poet mixes drinks out of wild liquors and is perpetually surprised that no one staggers.

Poetry can be heard at manholes, echoing up Dante's fire escape.

It recognizes the totalitarianism of the rational mind and breaks through it.

A poem is a dinghy setting out to sea from the listing ship of society.

A poem is a shadow of a plane fleeing over the ground like a cross escaping a church.

The poem is a telescope waiting for the poet to focus it.

Every poet his own priest and his own confessor.

Poetry is at once sacred and pagan play.

Poetry is play at its most utopian.

Poetry the ludic play of *homo ludens.*

Poetry a fornication against fate.

It is the humming of moths as they circle the flame.

It is the moon weeping because it must fade away in the day.

It is a wood boat moored in the shade under a weeping willow in the bend of a river.

The poet sees eternity in the mute eyes of all animals, including men and women.

Poetry is the real subject of great prose.

It speaks the unspeakable. It utters the inutterable sigh of the heart.

Each poem a momentary madness, and the unreal is the realist.

Poetry a form of lyric insanity.

A poem is still a knock on a door of the unknown.

A poem a piercing look into the very heart of things.

It is a realization of the subjective, the inner life of being.

Art is not Chance. Chance is not art, except by chance.

Great poets are the antennae of the race, with more than rabbit ears.

Poetry the ultimate illusion to live by.

Like a breast, a poem is more beautiful if it is veiled in mystery.

A poet a trance-dancer in the Last Waltz.

Poetry assuages our absolute loneliness in the lonely universe.

The light we see in the sky comes from a distant burning, as does poetry.

Poetry is a radical presence constantly goading us.

Poetry in handcuffs handcuffs the human race.

Poetry can still save the world by transforming consciousness.

A sunflower maddened with light sheds the seeds of poems.

In poetry, trees, beasts, and humans talk.

Poetry gives voice to all who see and sing and cry and laugh.

A poem is a window through which everything that passes can be seen anew.

Each poem a passion fruit, a pith of pure being.

Eyes & lips the doors of love, sight & sound the portals of poetry.

The kind sun of Impressionism makes poems out of light and shade. The broken light of abstract expressionism makes poems out of chaos.

Images appear and disappear in poetry and painting, out of a dark void and into it again, messengers of light and rain, raising their bright flickered lamps and vanishing in an instant. Yet they can be glimpsed long enough to save them as shadows on a wall in Plato's cave.

Just as the soul of civilization is seen in its architecture, a paucity of poetic imagination signals the decline of its culture.

The war against the imagination is not the only war. Using the 9/11 Twin Towers disaster as an excuse, America has initiated the Third World War, which is the War against the Third World.

Stutterers and stammerers also have the right to make poetry.

Poetry is a plant that grows at night to give name to desire.

Poetry a mediation between every-day reality and us.

Poetry about poetry is counterfeit poetry.

Poetry a meditation that assuages the loneliness of the long-distance swimmer.

Non-psychedelic poetry can enlighten a psychedelic.

Poetry eats Proust's cookies and washes its mouth with song.

Poetry destroys the bad breath of machines.

Poetry a pure parallel universe.

Poetry has no gender but isn't sexless.

Poetry is both the dough and the leaven.

Poetry the camera-eye of the mind, without a shutter.

Poetry exists because some men try to put flowers in prison.

Any child who can catch a firefly owns poetry.

The lyric surge and strife of life is poetry.

Poetry an innate urge toward truth and beauty.

When poets are treated like dogs, they howl.

Speech is to poetry as sound is to music, and it must sing.

Poetry is making something out of nothing, and it can be about nothing and still mean something.

The function of poetry is to debunk with light.

Poetry like love dies hard among the ruins.

Poetry like love a natural painkiller. The label on the bottle says: "Restores wonder and innocence."

The poet a membrane to filter light and disappear in it.

Poetry is a handprint of the invisible, a footprint of visible reality, following it like a shadow.

Poetry a timeless tick, a beat of the heart in timeless eternity.

As long as there is an unknown, there will be poetry.

Poetry a shining spear for the poorest warrior.

Love delights in love. Joy delights in joy. Poetry delights in poetry.

Great poetry requires *hunger and passion.*

The greatest poem is lyric life itself.

Poetry is making love on hot after-noons in Montana.

Poetry is the earth turning and turn-ing, with its humans every day turn-ing into light or darkness.

La vida es sueño. Life is a real dream and poetry dreams it.

But poetry serves many masters, not all beatific. Every age gets the poetry it deserves.

Eyes are stars; stars are eyes looking down at us with indifference, the blind eyes of nature.

There are three kinds of poetry:

Supine poetry accepts the status quo. Sitting poetry written by the sitting establishment has a bottom line dictated by its day job. Standing poetry is the poetry of commitment, sometimes great, sometimes dreadful.

The idea of poetry as an arm of class war disturbs the sleep of those who do not wish to be disturbed in the pursuit of happiness.

The poet by definition is the bearer of Eros and love and freedom and thus the natural-born *non-violent* enemy of any police state.

It is the ultimate Resistance.

The poet a subversive barbarian at the city gates, *non-violently* challenging the toxic status quo.

Dissident poetry is not UnAmerican.

The highest poetry is saying we might die without it.

It can salvage deeply tragic lives.

It is the voice within the voice of the turtle.

It is the face behind the face of the race.

It is the voice of the Fourth Person Singular.

Poetry the last lighthouse in rising seas.

FORETHOUGHTS

POPULIST MANIFESTO #1

(1976)

Poets, come out of your closets,
Open your windows, open your doors,
You have been holed-up too long
in your closed worlds.
Come down, come down
from your Russian Hills and Telegraph
    Hills,
your Beacon Hills and your Chapel
    Hills,
your Mount Analogues and
    Montparnasses,
down from your foot hills and
    mountains,
out of your tepees and domes.
The trees are still falling
and we'll to the woods no more.
No time now for sitting in them

As man burns down his own house
to roast his pig.
No more chanting Hare Krishna
while Rome burns.
San Francisco's burning,
Mayakovsky's Moscow's burning
the fossil-fuels of life.
Night & the Horse approaches
eating light, heat & power,
and the clouds have trousers.
No time now for the artist to hide
above, beyond, behind the scenes,
indifferent, paring his fingernails,
refining himself out of existence.
No time now for our little literary
     games,
no time now for our paranoias &
     hypochondrias,
no time now for fear & loathing,
time now only for light & love.
We have seen the best minds of our
     generation

destroyed by boredom at poetry
    readings.
Poetry isn't a secret society,
It isn't a temple either.
Secret words & chants won't do any
    longer.
The hour of *om*ing is over,
the time for keening come,
time for keening & rejoicing
over the coming end
of industrial civilization
which is bad for earth & Man.
Time now to face outward
in the full lotus position
with eyes wide open,
Time now to open your mouths
with a new open speech,
time now to communicate with all
    sentient beings,
All you poets of the cities
hung in museums, including myself,
All you poet's poets writing poetry
    about poetry,

All you dead language poets and
     deconstructionists,
All you poetry workshop poets
in the boondock heart of America,
All you house-broken Ezra Pounds,
All you far-out freaked-out cut-up
     poets,
All you pre-stressed Concrete poets,
All you cunnilingual poets,
All you pay-toilet poets groaning with
     graffitti,
All you A-train swingers who never
     swing on birches,
All you masters of the sawmill haiku
in the Siberias of America,
All you eyeless unrealists,
All you self-occulting supersurrealists,
All you bedroom visionaries
and closet agitpropagators,
All you Groucho Marxist poets
and leisure-class Comrades
who lie around all day

and talk about the workingclass
    proletariat,
All you Catholic anarchists of poetry,
All you Black Mountaineers of poetry,
All you Boston Brahmins and Bolinas
    bucolics,
All you den mothers of poetry,
All you zen brothers of poetry,
All you suicide lovers of poetry,
All you hairy professors of poesie,
All you poetry reviewers
drinking the blood of the poet,
All you Poetry Police—
Where are Whitman's wild children,
where the great voices speaking out
with a sense of sweetness and sublimity,
where the great new vision,
the great world-view,
the high prophetic song
of the immense earth
and all that sings in it
And our relation to it—

Poets, descend
to the street of the world once more
And open your minds & eyes
with the old visual delight,
Clear your throat and speak up,
Poetry is dead, long live poetry
with terrible eyes and buffalo strength.
Don't wait for the Revolution
or it'll happen without you,
Stop mumbling and speak out
with a new wide-open poetry
with a new commonsensual 'public
    surface'
with other subjective levels
or other subversive levels,
a tuning fork in the inner ear
to strike below the surface.
Of your own sweet Self still sing
yet utter 'the word en-masse'—
Poetry the common carrier
for the transportation of the public
to higher places

than other wheels can carry it.
Poetry still falls from the skies
into our streets still open.
They haven't put up the barricades,
     yet,
the streets still alive with faces,
lovely men & women still walking
     there,
still lovely creatures everywhere,
in the eyes of all the secret of all
still buried there,
Whitman's wild children still sleeping
     there,
Awake and sing in the open air.

POPULIST MANIFESTO #2

(1978)

Sons of Whitman sons of Poe
sons of Lorca & Rimbaud
or their dark daughters
poets of another breath
poets of another vision
Who among you still speaks of
    revolution
Who among you still unscrews
the locks from the doors
in this revisionist decade?
'You are President of your own body,
    America'
Thus spoke Kush in Tepotzlan
youngblood wildhaired angel poet
one of a spawn of wild poets
in the image of Allen Ginsberg
wandering the wilds of America

'You Rimbauds of another breath'
sang Kush
and wandered off with his own
    particular paranoias
maddened like most poets
for one mad reason or another
in the unmade bed of the world
Sons of Whitman
in your 'public solitude'
bound by blood-duende
'President of your own body America'
Take it back from those who have
    maddened you
back from those who stole it
and steal it daily
The subjective must take back the
    world
from the objective gorillas & guerrillas
    of the world
We must rejoin somehow
the animals in the fields
in their steady-state meditation

'Your life is in your own hands still
Make it flower make it sing'
(so sang mad Kush in Tepotzlan)
'a constitutional congress of the body'
still to be convened to seize control
of the State
the subjective state
from those who have subverted it
The arab telephone of the avant-garde
has broken down
And I speak to you now
from another country
Do not turn away
in your public solitudes
you poets of other visions
of the separate lonesome visions
untamed uncornered visions
fierce recalcitrant visions
you Whitmans of another breath
which is not the too-cool breath of
    modern poetry
which is not the halitosis of industrial
    civilization

Listen now Listen again
to the song in the blood the dark
    duende a dark singing
between the tickings of civilization
between the lines of its headlines
in the silences between cars
driven like weapons
In two hundred years of freedom
we have invented
the permanent alienation of the
    subjective
almost every truly creative being
alienated & expatriated
in his own country
in Middle America or San Francisco
the death of the dream in your birth
o meltingpot America
I speak to you
from another country
another kind of blood-letting land
from Tepotzlan the poet's lan'
Land of the Lord of the Dawn
                    Quetzalcoatl

Land of the Plumed Serpent
I signal to you
as Artaud signaled
through the flames
I signal to you
over the heads of the land
the hard heads that stand like menhirs
above the land in every country
the short-haired hyenas
who still rule everything
I signal to you from Poets' Land
you poets of the alienated breath
to take back your land again
and the deep sea of the subjective
Have you heard the sound of the ocean
    lately
the sound by which daily
the stars still are driven
the sound by which nightly
the stars retake their sky
The sea thunders still to remind you
of the thunder in the blood
to remind you of your selves

Think now of your self
as of a distant ship
Think now of your beloved
of the eyes of your beloved
whoever is most beloved
he who held you hard in the dark
or she who washed her hair by the
    waterfall
whoever makes the heart pound
the blood pound
Listen says the river
Listen says the sea Within you
you with your private visions
of another reality a separate reality
Listen and study the charts of time
Read the sanskrit of ants in the sand
You Whitmans of another breath
there is no one else to tell
how the alienated generations
have lived out their expatriate visions
here and everywhere
The old generations have lived them
    out

Lived out the bohemian myth in
    Greenwich Villages
Lived out the Hemingway myth
in *The Sun Also Rises*
at the Dôme in Paris
or with the bulls at Pamplona
Lived out the Henry Miller myth
in the *Tropics* of Paris
and the great Greek dream
of *The Colossus of Maroussi*
and the tropic dream of Gauguin
Lived out the D. H. Lawrence myth
in *The Plumed Serpent*
in Mexico Lake Chapala
And the Malcolm Lowry myth
Under the Volcano at Cuernavaca
And then the saga of *On the Road*
and the Bob Dylan myth Blowing in
    the Wind
How many roads must a man walk
    down
How many Neal Cassadys on lost
    railroad tracks

How many replicas of Woody Guthrie
    with cracked guitars
How many photocopies of longhaired
    Joan
How many Ginsberg facsimiles and
    carbon-copy Keseys
still wandering the streets of America
in old tennis shoes and backpacks
or driving beat-up school buses
with destination-signs reading 'Further'
How many Buddhist Catholics how
    many cantors
chanting the Great Paramita Sutra
on the Lower East Side
How many Whole Earth Catalogs
lost in outhouses on New Mexico
    communes
How many Punk Rockers waving
    swastikas
Franco is dead but so is Picasso
Chaplin is dead but I'd wear his bowler
having outlived all our myths but his
the myth of the pure subjective

the collective subjective
the Little Man in each of us
waiting with Charlot or Pozzo
On every corner I see them
those lost subjective selves
hidden inside their tight clean clothes
Their hats are not derbys they have no
    canes
They turn and hitch their pants
and walk away from us
in the great American night

(Tepotzlan–San Francisco)

MODERN POETRY IS PROSE

(1978)

I am thumbing through a great anthology
of contemporary poetry, and it would
seem that "the voice that is great within
us" sounds within us mostly in a prose
voice, albeit in the typography of poetry.
Which is not to say it is prosaic or has no
depths, which is not to say it is dead or
dying, or not lovely or not beautiful or
not well written or not witty and brave.
It is very much alive, very well written,
lovely, lively prose—prose that stands
without the crutches of punctuation,
prose whose syntax is so clear it can be
written all over the page, in open forms
and open fields, and still be very clear,
very dear prose. And in the typography
of poetry, the poetic and the prosaic intellect masquerade in each other's clothes.

Walking through our prose buildings in the 21st century, one may look back and wonder at this strange age which allowed poetry to walk in prose rhythms and still called it poetry. Modern poetry is prose because it sounds as subdued as any city man or woman whose life force is submerged in urban life. Modern poetry is prose because it doesn't have much *duende*, dark spirit of earth and blood, no soul of dark song, no passion musick. Like modern sculpture, it loves the concrete. Like minimal art, it minimizes emotion in favor of understated irony and implied intensity. As such it is the perfect poetry for technocratic man. But how often does this poetry rise above the mean sea level of his darkling plain? Ezra Pound once decanted his opinion that only in times of decadence does poetry separate itself from music. And this is the way the world ends, not with a song but a whimper.

Eighty or ninety years ago, when all the machines began to hum, almost (as it seemed) in unison, the speech of man certainly began to be affected by the absolute staccato of machines. And city poetry certainly echoed it. Whitman was a holdover, singing the song of himself. And Sandburg a holdover, singing his sagas. And Vachel Lindsay a holdover, drumming his chants. And later there was Wallace Stevens with his harmonious "fictive music." And there was Langston Hughes. And Allen Ginsberg, chanting his mantras, singing Blake. There still are others everywhere, jazz poets and poetic strummers and wailers in the streets of the world, making poetry out of the urgent insurgent Now, of the immediate instant self, the incarnate carnal self (as D. H. Lawrence called it).

But much poetry was caught up in the linotype's hot slug and now in the computer's so cold type. No song among the typists, no song in our concrete architecture, our concrete music. And the nightingales may still be singing near the Convent of the Sacred Heart, but we can hardly hear them in the city waste lands of T. S. Eliot, nor in his *Four Quartets* (which can't be played on any instrument and yet is the most beautiful prose of our time). Nor in the prose wastes of Ezra Pound's *Cantos* which aren't *canti* because they couldn't possibly be sung. Nor in the pangolin prose of Marianne Moore (who called her writing poetry for lack of anything better to call it). Nor in the great prose blank verse of Karl Shapiro's *Essay on Rime*, nor in the outer city speech of William Carlos Williams, in the flat-out speech of his *Paterson*. All of which is applauded by poetry professors and poetry reviewers in all the best places, none of whom will commit the original sin of saying some poet's poetry is prose in the typography of poetry—just as the poet's friends will never tell him, just as the poet's editors will never say it—the dumbest conspiracy of silence in the history of letters.

Most modern poetry is poetic prose but it is saying plenty, by its own example, about what death of the spirit our technocratic civilization may be dealing us, enmeshed in machines and macho nationalisms, while some continue longing for some nightingale among the pines of Respighi. It is the bird singing that makes us happy.

BIBLIOGRAPHICAL NOTE

After a lifetime, this (r)evolutionary little book is still a work-in-progress, the poet's ars poetica, to which at 88 he is constantly adding.

The earliest version of "What Is Poetry" was transcribed from a KPFA (FM) broadcast by the author in the late 1950s; it was republished in various versions in newspapers, small press editions and translations. A small part of "What Is Poetry?" was published in *Americus, Book I*, Section III (New Directions, 2004). "Populist Manifesto # 1" was broadcast in 1975 and published in *The New York Times* as "Popular Manifesto." It had its first book publication in *Who Are We Now?* (New Directions, 1976); "Populist Manifesto # 2 (also known as "Adieu à Charlot") was published in the *Los Angeles Times* in 1978 and had its first book publication in *Landscapes of Living and Dying* (New Directions, 1979). "Modern Poetry Is Prose" was published in *Endless Life* (New Directions, 1981).